Budgeting 101

By Kirk G. Meyer

Budgeting 101

Copyright © 2014 by Kirk G. Meyer

Disclaimer: Every effort was made to describe the information in this book in an accurate manner as of the publication date. The author makes no guarantees regarding the information in this book.

Why I Wrote this booklet

I wrote this booklet to share my knowledge and experience with budgets and how they are the building block to healthy finances. If you are not aware of where your hard-earned money is going, then you will never be able to save or know where your money is going. By budgeting, you will be able to answer most of the questions you will have concerning your finances. These are things that everyone needs to know, and that is why I wrote Budgeting 101.

Why You Should Buy this booklet

Anyone who is old enough to earn some money needs to know and understand the importance of budgets. Without budgets, there is little to no chance that you will be able to stay on top of your finances. Budgets allow us to know how much money is coming in through jobs or any other source. Budgets allow you to figure out then the outflows of money and, more importantly, where those funds go. Only by knowing these things will you know where you stand with your finances. This booklet explains the budgeting process and provides you some places where you can get sample budget formats if you do not want to create your own. Get on top of your finances today and read this booklet.

My GIFT to You!

As a big thank you for getting Budgeting 101, I want to offer you some valuable gifts and a chance to get some on-going financial advice. Just for getting this book, it entitles you to my Budget Spreadsheet and Debt Reduction Spreadsheet that I normally sell for a total of $10. It is yours free for getting Budgeting 101 and signing up for my free email newsletters that have previews to my books. These special articles are geared towards personal finance and now access to these two useful spreadsheets. To get your spreadsheets now, go to my blog's website and sign up today. Visit www.kgmeyerpc.com today to get your free valuable spreadsheets.

Table of Contents

Budgeting Basics

A budget is simply the process of projecting future income and expenses over a specified period. They are viewed as a roadmap of one's patterns of spending as well as saving. If a person does not know and understand where the money is spent, it is almost impossible to save properly. And to be honest, most Americans are not savers by any sense of the term because they tend to spend more than they earn. The key to avoiding the American spend- more-than-you-earn pitfall is to take the time and make a budget, so it is possible to know where one's hard-earned money goes during each period in the budget. A well-developed budget can aid a person or family in planning expenditures, help pay bills promptly, help to save for an emergency fund or achieve larger goals such as a down payment on a house, a child's education, and especially retirement.

Most already know the basics of making budgets, but where some people seem to fall short is in the implementation or execution of the budgeting process. The best way to develop and follow a budget is to approach it as a living, breathing document. Let us face it, and no one can prepare a budget at the beginning of the year with 100% accuracy, because first, no one can predict the future, and second, things in life happen. That is why it is important to understand that a budget acts as a roadmap to one's finances and is not set in stone. Luckily in today's world, there are several options available to aid and assist in budgeting. Some prefer a spreadsheet to track their finances. Others may prefer a Web-based budgeting software system. Still, others might prefer a site that has been created to follow all things financial, basically combining a balance sheet and income statement in one location. Others prefer older methods such as tracking things in a notebook or using the cash envelop system. We will take a look at all of these options later in the booklet. There is not a single right answer to how a budget needs to be created or tracked. The important thing is that a budget is established and used in some manner.

As the title of this section implies, some areas are considered budget basics. In the simplest terms, you can break a budget down into three components. But before developing a budget or budget plan, it is first important to track all expenses for a minimum of two, or preferably three, months to have a clear idea where the money is going, while also examining sources of income. The easier of these two aspects of budgeting is the tracking of income, as most have only one or two sources of income that will be the basis of the budget. Some people in retirement may have several sources of income considering social security, pensions, or other retirement accounts. Unless your budget takes taxes, insurance, and other payroll deductions into consideration, it is best to use the net income for budgeting purposes. If there is an insurance expense not accounted for in your payroll deductions, make sure to include it as an expense. It is also important to make sure all sources of income are listed, as a clear picture of the funding that will be made available for expenses is crucial. Now that you have tracked as all of your expenses over a two or three month period, it will be fairly easy to estimate what one can expect to spend on various expense categories. Some expenses are considered fixed, such as a mortgage. Others may have a fixed frequency but variable amounts, such as a utility bill that is due each month, the same as a mortgage, but for varying amounts, based on the amount of water or electricity used for the month.

Finally, there are truly flexible expenses such as entertainment that will vary in both frequency and amount. Avoid credit card debt to the best of your ability, and they are also considered a variable expense. Whatever the difference is between the total income and total expenses, hopefully, is excess income used for savings. But as it was pointed out earlier in this section, most American budgets run a deficit, meaning expenses exceed income.

Now that we have explained the three basic components of the budget, it is important to find a monitoring method that works best for each situation. While all the examples mentioned earlier will work, it will depend on what is most comfortable for you, the user. While some may like the ease of a spreadsheet, others may prefer a system that is a web-based program accessed from any computer with Internet access. And the extremely serious budgeter can utilize the most comprehensive method recommended, which is a total financial review of one's situation.

Budgeting 101

It does not matter if you are a young individual or a couple just starting, an established family that is about to have children enter college, older adults about to start what everyone hopes are a long retirement or individuals who are already well into their retirement years. Anyone in these situations, or at any other point in life, needs to have a budget to understand where all of their hard-earned money goes. A budget is not a tool that is meant to restrict one's actions but rather used to help explain one's financial situation in life. Budgets tell us if we are living within our means and thereby able to save any excess income; they will also tell whether someone is just breaking even or simply living day to day by taking on extra debt. Without the use of a budget, these answers will go unanswered, and any financial planning may be in vain.

At first, the idea of creating a budget may seem like a tedious exercise in one's financial affairs. This may especially be true if you already have a good sense of your financial situation, and the thought of spending time on a budget may seem unnecessary. However,

11

budgets are valuable tools, not just to those who may not have large quantities of money, but also to people who are operating with an excess of income. A well thought out budget can keep spending on track and even help uncover areas where you waste money or instances where better uses of the funds if diverted to another category in the budget.

Before you get too worried about what a budget is or will mean to you, the important thing is to stop procrastinating and begin the process of developing a workable budget. Creating one's first budget is the hardest part of the entire budgeting process. After you create the initial budget, all that you have to do is make changes that allow you to operate within boundaries while still being able to enjoy life. A budget does not mean the end of fun for an individual or a family; it simply means developing a system by which everyone involved can live with and follow. All it takes is a few minutes to create a simple budget, and it is wise to add and subtract things as situations arise that may affect the budget. After you create the basic budget and established, it is best to track all income and expenses for two to three months to be able to get an average of what a year's worth of budgeting would look like. After you do that, take some time and create a more comprehensive budget that covers all aspects of your income and expenses.

Now that you created a basic budget and figures have supported all categories, it is time to start using the basic budget while creating a more comprehensive one that will detail the situation better and more clearly. After all, spending a lot of time creating a solid budget to be followed, so it is worth the effort to persevere and stick to it. Do not be distracted from the budget that was created and do not fall into the trap where, after several months, creating the budget is not being put it to use. One way to ensure that the budget is practical and feasible is to keep it somewhat simple. Do not overthink the situation but do try to encompass all areas where you spend money. One way to keep it simple is to use a spreadsheet that tracks income and expenses over several categories. An inexpensive spreadsheet is available through my blog's website by clicking this link, https://bit.ly/3mAScDl. If that spreadsheet is not what you need, there are many options available on the

Internet simply by searching for a "budget spreadsheet" in any search engine.

For those of you who want a spreadsheet-based program that has cloud storage for a nominal extra charge, you may want to consider the following. I found this software several years ago and based my above spreadsheet off of it to a degree, but at the time could not remember the name of the firm that I bought it from. Well, Simple Planning offers a bundle of spreadsheets that will enable you to track your mortgage, 401(k), investments, and much more all for one low price, and it offers Cloud storage for a minimal charge that comes with any updates. To see this magnificent set of spreadsheets, please visit https://bit.ly/2HR3QeE. If a web-based budgeting system is preferred that is still simple to use and is accessible from any computer connected to the Internet, I have found this to be reasonably priced and very useful in making budgets easy to understand and follow.

If you prefer the old fashion manner of budgeting, I have created a printable PDf that will allow you to track off of your income and expenses in one location. To purchase this useful PDF, go to]https://bit.ly/2Gf5czi. I also offer a set of budgeting cash envelopes that can aid and assist in your budgeting process at http://bit.ly/2LoO6id. Later in the booklet, we will examine a free tool that is a comprehensive approach to budgeting and debt management, and which also includes a balance sheet option for summarizing assets.

If you overspend your budget in one area, that is cause to re-evaluate the budget. Budgets tell the story of how you spend money in any particular area. If overspending routinely occurs in one area, it would make sense that spending must be reduced in another area to keep the budget balanced. It is easy to tell when overspend occurs in the area, as the budget tools mentioned in this section will show all categories and if they have been over- or under-spent. By glancing at the budget, you can tell at any moment where the budget stands with overall spending. Overspending is not necessarily a bad thing, depending on the underlying cause, which will need to be examined and re-evaluated. One possibility is that the budget was flawed from the beginning and thereby not realistic. Another is that things happen in life, and unexpected events will always occur at one point in time or another. The key is to understand the category that was overspent and why. Once that is done, it is easy to get the budget back on track. One way to compensate for emergencies is by having an emergency fund for such occasions. But let's be clear on this point, learning to identify what are actual emergencies is paramount; for example, needing new tires is not an emergency, but an expense accounted for in the budget. A real emergency would be that the transmission on the car went out unexpectedly and must be repaired or replaced. That is not routine maintenance on a car, whereas a new set of tires is.

One of the best ways to keep on a budget is by not using credit or debit cards for purchases. There is an old saying that "cash is king," and by using cash, people are less likely to overspend on item categories when they are shopping. For those items that are cash-oriented like gas, lunch, and groceries, set aside a designated amount of cash at the beginning of each week in your cash envelopes, and when the money runs out, you know that you are done spending in that areas until the next week. Many systems have been advocated by various financial experts on how to survive on a cash budget, with possibly the easiest to use and maintain is the cash envelope system that is promoted by Dave Ramsey. In Dave's personal finance books, he suggests placing the budgeted cash amount for each week in an envelope marked with that category. When the cash runs out of that envelope, spending from that category ceases.

In this section, we have looked at the basics of Budgeting 101 and how to begin the process. At this point, options for budgeting range for some simple to medium to complex budgets for you to select. The most important thing to remember about creating and using a budget is to make one that works for the situation intended for, and secondly, to be diligent using and follow that budget. As I pointed out earlier, you need to remember that budgets are living and breathing documents that require adjustments as the situation warrants.

How to Begin

Getting started may be easier for some than for others. If someone organized, starting a budget will be easier than for those who have no idea of where they stand financially. Likewise, for those who balance their checkbooks regularly, they will, in theory, have a better idea of their income and, to some extent, their expenses. Again, it is a good idea to track all of the income and expenses for at least two, but preferably three months so to paint t an accurate picture for the budget. Without doing this preliminary work, a budget will not be very meaningful or relevant.

First, you must know the sources and amounts of income to be budgeted. If paid monthly, semi-monthly, or every two weeks, it is important to know what amount you will "net," or bring home after taxes and other payroll deductions are accounted from your paycheck. This is the first level of the foundation for a budget, a stable and reliable source of income. Also, it is important to track and account for any irregular income that may be received in a period or over a month or year. This can be a one-time income in the form of a bonus or cash gifts received for such occasions as birthday, graduation, or marriage. For a budget to be as accurate as possible, it is necessary to account for all income and from all sources.

The next step is to create some lists or categories of expenses. There are two types of expenses, the first of which is necessary or non-discretionary. The necessary are expenses such as mortgage or rent, auto, and home insurance, any health insurance or costs, repayments for legal loan obligations, utilities, and groceries, to name a few. The second type of expense includes those who are not considered necessary and are discretionary. These expenses include things such as entertainment, eating out, vacations, and gifts, to name a few. It is important to note that most non-discretionary expenses occur regularly, such as monthly, but what is also worth noting is that the amount paid every time the expense is due may fluctuate to some degree. A mortgage, for a smart homeowner, is either a 15 or 30-year fixed mortgage where the payment is stable and consistent from month to month. While these payments may vary to a degree, it is due to changes in things such as the cost of insurance or taxes, and it generally will only change the payment on an annual basis. An example of other non-discretionary expenses that are paid monthly but may not be the same each month is utilities. Consider a natural gas bill, if that is an expense for budgeting purposes. It stands to reason that in most areas, a natural gas bill will be much higher in the winter months when the heat is needed, as compared to the summer months when electricity is used more for air conditioning, and natural gas use is limited. Credit card payments may vary from month to month, but after beginning a budget regimen and with some simple planning, credit cards will not be used at all or will be paid off in full every month. Later in the booklet, we will examine debt reduction, in combination with the use of budgets.

Now that you accounted for all of the discretionary and non-discretionary expenses, it is time to set up the budget. Now here is where some individual input and careful thought will be required. When tracking the first three months of the year to set up a budget, it will likely have to be adjusted. For example, if the budget has a category for gifts, most consumers will spend most of their gift budget in the latter part of the year to purchase Christmas gifts. Insurance premiums also are not always paid monthly. If, for example, auto insurance was not paid in the three months that initially tracked in the setup phase, the insurance budget will need to be adjusted accordingly. Utilities are the last example of items that may require an adjustment when budgeting. Someone who lives in the north will have much higher natural gas bills in the winter months, as compared to someone who lives in the south. And the reverse is true to a degree; those living in the south should, in theory, have higher electricity bills in the summer months compared to someone living in the north. After budgeting for an entire year, the following budgets can be created more easily by taking all of a category's expenses and dividing the total by twelve for a monthly average.

If at this point, the expenses exceed the income, it is time to examine all of the expenses that are listed. First, start with the discretionary expenses, as they are not technically required. While it is still important to be able to live, have fun, and enjoy one's life, you must live within your means. If your budget is in the red, it is time to start cutting. If someone is a working member of the family and eats out every day for lunch, to reduce that expense, you can bring a packed lunch from home instead of eating out with colleagues. Another area of discretionary spending that is easy to cut is entertainment. Is it necessary to have the premium channels on one's cable or satellite package? Try reducing the entertainment package on your television service and consider utilizing Netflix streaming service for under $15 a month. Compare that to the $50 plus a month some premium channel packages can cost through pay television. If the budget is in the red, it is time to look at every discretionary expense and be honest as to whether the expense is necessary, or can be reduced or cut out altogether.

If the budget is still in the red or just barely in the black, positive, begin to look at non-discretionary expenses for further cuts. Now, this area is a little tougher to cut, but it can be done and done efficiently if the situation is dire and requires serious actions. If someone has a mortgage, there is little to reduce the monthly expense without refinancing the entire mortgage. Refinancing can be advantageous if interest rates have fallen since the mortgage was taken out and can reduce the expense; however, in the case of a mortgage that has been in place for several years, it does no good to refinance a new 30-

year mortgage even if it is at a lower interest rate unless refinanced with a shorter term or the closing costs can be paid in cash. By doing this, you save significantly every month, but in the bigger picture paying interest on a mortgage for 15 years is a very significant saving over refinancing into a new 30-year mortgage with a full 30 years of interest payments. If you have an expensive car and a loan on that car, there is no reason not to sell the car and buy one that is more affordable or even one paid for with cash. In the event you can own your cars, it may be wise to continue to pay yourself a monthly "car payment" that can be used for automotive repairs as they arise or even save to buy your next car outright when it is time to replace the current one. Cars are an asset that depreciates at a rapid rate and, therefore, an unwise loan or debt to carry. Utilities are another area of non-discretionary expenses to examine to look for savings. Use common sense when setting the thermostat. For example, if you are cold in the winter, it is more cost-effective to put on extra clothes rather than turn up the thermostat. The same is true for the summer; dress in cooler clothes, use ceiling fans, or look for other ways to ensure that the house is as energy-efficient as possible.

Now at this point, it is hopeful that the budget is in the black, meaning that the difference between income and expenses is positive. If a budget results in positive cash flow, it allows the individual or family the ability to save or to accumulate wealth. There are numerous things that most people will encounter in life that require large outlays of money. The key is to budget for these expenses and plan in advance for them as much as possible. Vacations are a good example. Do not use credit cards to finance a family trip, as that may result in the trip costing much more than originally planned. Unless you pay off the credit card balance in full at the end of the billing cycle, it could take months or years to pay off the vacation, only to waste hard-earned money on excessive interest charges. If there are children in the family who would like to go to college, it is appropriate to have savings for college as a monthly expense from the beginning, and not to view this as a simple savings need. This is similar to the earlier example of a paid-off car while continuing to "pay" a monthly car payment. At some point, you will need a new car, so continue to treat the car payment as an expense, and when the time comes, a new car can be paid for with cash or require a minuscule amount financed. College expenses are similar, and it is better to factor them into the budget as expenses and save properly, instead of waiting until the child is in high school to begin saving. Both of these examples show the wisdom of having the money and not needing it as compared to needing it and not having anything saved. Retirement is something that should not be considered savings, but rather a necessity for anyone in today's America. When making a budget or values-based financial plan, it is imperative to fund retirement, think of it as paying yourself, first and foremost. Actual savings are for things like a down payment on a house for someone who rents. A down payment on a car if someone is buying a new one. Any vacations planned, and anything that is not considered a necessity and is not within your financial means at present.

You can break savings down into three major types: short-term, medium-term, and long-term goals. Here is where I differ from many individuals who teach or suggest budgeting methodology, and I will explain as these areas. First, we will consider a short-term savings

Budgeting 101 by Kirk G. Meyer

goal, which would include such things as car repairs or family vacations. These are typically expenses spent in 24 months or less. A medium-term goal is generally one of between two years and about five years before being paid. These types of expenses generally include such things as a wedding, a new car, or college expenses, depending on the current age(s) of the children. Long-term goals can be fairly tricky to plan for. As I stated earlier in this section, I view retirement and savings for a child's education not only as a possible long-term goal but as one that is viewed as a non-discretionary expense. Saving in one's company 401(k) plan, too many is a necessity and not considered savings as much as it is an expense. The same can be said about an individual retirement account (IRA), as it is always important to pay yourself first out of every paycheck. But when choosing to save between a 401(k) and an individual retirement account, the 401(k) is deducted right from the paycheck, and it is money never seen in your bank account. It is an automatic savings plan and one where you rarely miss the money. Any savings in an individual retirement account, while good and necessary, does not carry the convenience of an automatic deduction, unless set up to be handled in such a manner. These savings and any others are intended for one's retirement are indeed long-term in nature.

Now that we have examined in more detail the "how-to" aspect of making a budget that works, the key is to follow and use the budget as intended. Making a budget and then not following it does no one any good. Unless you know where the funds come from and where they go, you will never win the battle over your finances. To complete this step in the budget process, the following items will be needed: pay stubs, credit card statements, bank statements, and a list of all-cash purchases for the three months used as the basis for the budget.

Ways to Ensure Success

Just because you take the time to create a budget, go through your expenses, and look for ways to reduce expenses and save, does not guarantee you will have a successful time at budgeting, especially the first time around. There are a few things that you can do that will help ensure the success of your budget and guide you in successful implementation. Do not look at budgeting as being set up to fail; rather, it is setting up a guide for the future, which will ultimately result in you taking control of your finances. One key to not failing in the budgeting process is to remember what has been previously stated in this booklet, that a budget is a living, breathing document intended to be changed and adapted to circumstances as life changes inevitably happen. By taking this approach to making and maintaining a budget, it is not set up to fail but rather to succeed and thrive.

An established budget will aid you in achieving your financial goals. To achieve these goals, you must determine to use the budget as intended to get to a place where the goals are made achievable. Here is the first key to the success of any budget: have a clear goal to work towards. Write the goal down and keep it in a place where they are visible. By having a clear goal and one written down, it will help keep you on track with your budget and will remind you why it is important. Goals such as "getting out of debt" or "managing money better" are worthy goals to strive towards, but a more realistic and achievable short-term goal is to create a budget that will enable you to save $100 a month or create six months' worth of emergency cash. While getting out of debt and saving $100 a month are both good goals, one is clear and precise, and the other is more general. If you were to take the goal of getting out of debt and break it down into smaller goals that are more specific and measurable, change it to "pay off all my credit card debts in the next two years." Then after that, you can have a new goal such as "paying off my student loans in the next five years." You still have the overall goal of getting out of debt, but it is now a series of smaller, more achievable goals. This is values-based planning, selecting goals that are achievable and based on your set of values and with a definite timeline to achieve them.

Budgeting 101 by Kirk G. Meyer

Make a budget as simple or as complex as it needs to be to fit your individual or family situation, and that will help achieve your financial goals. Some may not want thirty categories in which to track expenses, while others may want to know where every penny is being spent and on what. Both budgets can be appropriate, depending on the circumstances and desires of the person whose job it is to create and use the budget. Some budgets will be time-consuming, but appropriate for that individual or family. Others will only require a small amount of time to maintain. It all depends on what the particular user is comfortable in doing.

If possible, set the budget up to be automatic. While this is not for everyone, it is useful for someone who is very busy and does not have a lot of time to be inputting data into a budget. The site www.mint.com allows the user to link bank accounts and credit card accounts to the site for easy tracking of expenses. While this site will take transactions from individual accounts and place them into categories, it does not paint a complete picture. Anything purchased with cash is not accounted for on the Mint site, although any withdrawals will show up in the transactions. Another positive about the Mint site is that it allows the user to not only track accounts and expenses, but will also act as a balance sheet where it allows the user to link brokerage and retirement accounts, list the value of a residence and other assets to derive a net worth for the user. This is an addition and enhancement to a simple budget using one of the previously mentioned methods. Perhaps the best part of Mint is that currently, it is a free site maintained by Intuit, the makers of Quicken and TurboTax.

You base your budgets on any time frame that you see as appropriate. While most budgets are a monthly basis, many people find that this format may not fit their needs. Some people prefer a shorter time frame for their budget and may have it coincide with their pay schedule. If you are paid every two weeks, it may make more sense to have a budget that spans that two week period. If paid monthly, it may make more sense to have a budget that tracks that influx of income. Use whatever fits your situation best and then stick with that time frame for the best results.

As stated previously, budgets are not the end of your fun, but rather the beginning of understanding and financial freedom. If a budget is going to work properly, it needs to meet a few criteria. First, it needs to be realistic and achievable. If a budget does not meet these criteria, it is doomed to fail no matter how well-intentioned. The second aspect that is a must for a budget to be successful is that the budgeter needs to be completely honest about their financial situation. If you are accustomed to going to dinner with friends on the weekend, it is probably not realistic to vow that you will no longer go to dinner on the weekends, when in fact, you know that you will most likely continue the tradition. The better approach is to compromise—for example, instead of going to dinner every weekend, we will only go out to dinner with friends once a month. In that scenario, the fun associated with going to dinner with friends remains intact. Still, it is reduced from every weekend to a single weekend per month, resulting in what could be a substantial saving.

For a budget to be successful, it must meet the criteria discussed so far. One way to follow a budget is to build in a reward system after the budget's goals are met over a specified period. If you meet the budgeted targets, and you or your family was able to save the desired amount, it is not unreasonable to build in a reward. The reward can be something as simple as going to a new movie not planned or budgeted for, or it may be purchasing that new pair of running shoes you have had your eye on. The reward needs to be within reason, but also substantial enough to give the incentive to meet the budgeted goals.

Budget Alternative

Budgeters may encounter issues in preparing a budget, such as the appropriate percent of one's salary to go to a particular category. While there is no right or wrong answer to such questions, use the following as a basic guideline. Each person's situation is different, but overall most people have somewhat similar situations molded into the following. Consider that a budget is a balancing act, and that act must balance, or it runs the risk of not working properly. It is important to realize that you need to start a budget as soon as possible and to be proactive, and not as an emergency tool after spending and debt issues force you to adopt a budget created out of fear or urgency. If for some reason, the types of budgets mentioned earlier are not feasible or simply are not working, the following is an approach that can be tried instead of a traditional budget. This method simply places one's income into four equal buckets.

The first bucket is one that will get paid, no matter what, and that is the taxes owed on income earned, including federal, state, or local income taxes. It may also include state sales tax or property taxes. No matter where in

America one lives, there will be some form of taxes due on all income earned, so it is safe to place the first 25% of one's income in the tax bucket without even thinking about it. If for some reason, the taxes turn out to be less than the 25% allocated, it is like a bonus at the end of the year. Now, this 25% may not be all taxes, as it is safe to place any payroll deduction into this bucket. The reason for this is that the money is taken out for the employee's benefits is similar to taxes in that the money is taken out of the paycheck before actually hitting a checking or savings account.

Most financial planners state that between 20% and 30% of income will go towards housing. In this exercise, dedicate the second 25% bucket to housing costs. This category is going to be for the payment of a mortgage or for the rent on a primary residence used for the individual or family who created the budget. Unlike the previous category, this is one that will require someone writing a check to pay, so it will result in hurting a little bit more than the taxes. It is important that housing is limited to 25% so that we may continue with this form of a budget.

The third 25% bucket is geared towards the debts of the household, excluding the mortgage or rent. This bucket is to pay credit card balances, student loans, car loans, or any other type of legal debts that require payments. If, for some reason, the debt level goes over the 25% allocated to the servicing of debts, a more formal budget may be needed, so expenses are reduced that are not determined to be necessary. In today's American society, it is becoming more and more prevalent that households are indeed taking on more debt.

The fourth and final 25% bucket is for living expenses. This is a catchall bucket, as it will encompass everything from groceries to utilities, clothing, gifts, charitable contributions, and even one's savings. Within lies the issue with using a simple 25% bucket approach, as there is little room for error, and it may not be totally practical for everyone. But if a true budget is not in your future, this approach is better than nothing.

Now, if you think these percentages are not appropriate, that is fine except the first bucket, taxes. That bucket needs to remain at 25%, regardless of whatever the other three buckets may be, if someone can live on 20%

of their salary and utilize only 15% for debt payments because they choose to live well within their means, which leaves 40% for living expenses. It is how one chooses to live that drives the percentage allocated to each bucket. If one is not sure how much to allocate to each bucket in this exercise, it is still wise to track two to three months' worth of expenditures to create an accurate picture and will assist in the proper assignment of percentages to each bucket.

About Kirk G. Meyer

Kirk G. Meyer's educational and work background is relatively diverse. Currently, Kirk is working on his Doctorate in Business Administration from William Howard Taft University. Kirk has completed an MS in Financial Planning from Bentley University in suburban Boston, Massachusetts, and is now an investment advisor in the State of Tennessee in addition to working for the government in the area of contracts. Kirk also holds a BS in Business Administration from Haskell Indian Nations University in Lawrence, Kansas, and an MBA and MS in Accounting from Strayer University in Washington, DC. Before Kirk's current position, Kirk was a bank examiner for a federal regulatory agency. In addition to Kirk's education and work experience, he is also a registered independent life insurance agent in his home state of Tennessee, able to advise on various life insurance and annuity products to individuals and families in need of these types of services. Kirk's educational background and love of helping others make him an asset to those looking for assistance and guidance in financial and personal financial matters. Kirk resides in Nashville, Tennessee, with his lovely wife.

How to Contact Kirk G. Meyer

Feel free to email Kirk at kirk@kgmeyerpc.com.

Please follow Kirk's blog at www.kgmeyerpc.com, and he welcomes any comments or suggestions on how to make his blog or books better for you.

You can also follow Kirk on Twitter at @kirkgmeyer

You can follow Kirk on Facebook at www.facebook.com/kgmeyerpc

You can follow Kirk on LinkedIn at www.linkedin.com/in/kirkgmeyer

You can follow Kirk on Pinterest at https://www.pinterest.com/kirkgmeyer/

You can follow Kirk on Instagram at https://www.instagram.com/kirkgmeyer/

One Last Chance for the Free Gifts!

Again, as a big thank you for getting Budgeting 101, I want to offer you some valuable gifts and a chance to get some on-going financial advice. Just for getting this book, it entitles you to my Budget Spreadsheet and Debt Reduction Spreadsheet that I normally sell for a total of $10. It is yours free for getting Budgeting 101 and signing up for my free email newsletters that have previews to my book. These special articles are geared towards personal finance and now access to these two useful spreadsheets. To get your spreadsheets now, go to my blog's website and sign up today. Visit http://bit.ly/KGMLetter today to get your free valuable spreadsheets.

Other Books by Kirk G. Meyer

Thrift Savings Plan: A Practical Guide to the TSP

The Basics of Life Insurance

A Brief Overview of Annuities

Financial Plans: Just the Basics

Personal Finance: A Grouping of Financial Topics

Final Expense Insurance

Budgeting 101

The Basics of Life Insurance and Annuities Bundle

Your Credit Report and You

The Basics of Personal Finance

Investing 101: A Basic Guide to Investing for Beginners

How the Stock Market Operates

401(k) Retirement Loans: Loans that can cost you more than you know

Basics of Personal Finance: How to Maintain a Financial Strategy

101 Powerful Tips for Legally Improving Your Credit Score